THIRTY EIGHT POEMS

by

PENNETHORNE HUGHES

Thirty Eight Poems

by
PENNETHORNE HUGHES

Chosen and with a Foreword by
Geoffrey Grigson

Contributions from
John Betjeman & John Arlott

John Baker
5 ROYAL OPERA ARCADE, PALL MALL, LONDON SW1

© 1970 Estate of Charles James Pennethorne Hughes,
Geoffrey Grigson, John Betjeman and John Arlott
First published in 1970 by
JOHN BAKER PUBLISHERS LTD
5 Royal Opera Arcade, Pall Mall
London SW1

S.B.N. 212.98362.8

Printed in Great Britain by The Grange Press at Southwick, Sussex

CONTENTS

My thanks are offered to Geoffrey Grigson, not
only for his Foreword, but for all the work that he
put into choosing this handful of poems from
seven times as many.

D.C.R.W.

THE WRITER OF THESE POEMS

Pennethorne Hughes was a divided man, like many others, and many in particular in his middle class generation (he was born in 1907), a man endeavouring or tempted to discover what he was, yet inclined to turn away — to what image, to what highly ambiguous substance? — from such findings as he made; except, I would say, in a few of his poems.

He was the only child, or the only surviving child, of a Kentish parson who moved from parish to parish, ending up in Wiltshire. Born in the Isle of Wight, Pennethorne Hughes was even more the child of his mother, a Miss Pennethorne, granddaughter of Sir James Pennethorne the architect, who had married long ago a daughter ascribed politely to the more celebrated John Nash. Actually the daughter had come from the loins of the Prince Regent in conjunction with Mrs. Nash. So Pennethorne Hughes was of royal, if not entirely enviable descent; himself a rufous Hanoverian, tall and straight, with fair hair and blue eyes. He was much aware of this descent. Equally, in his envelope of parsonage (old middle class style), public school (where he boxed), and Oxford, he was aware of the scrupulous unease of the Thirties.

What ought he to believe? His clerical father's religion, established and respectable? No, and yes. He compromised. He wrote *Call to Prayer;* but then he liked evensong, and *Abide with Me,* and the blessing, and Tennysonian bells, lin-lan-lone. What should he do in this life? Teach? Enter the public service in some way? He compromised. For a while he taught in his old milieu. Then in the B.B.C., in its Talks Department, which avowed aims of public betterment and was attached more than a little to patronage, intellectual slumming and sentimentality, he remained in his old world of values, with a foot in something-on-the-way.

Where ought he to stand, brave boys, in politics and vis-á-vis society? Again he compromised. I first met him — a young talks producer from Bristol — in the company of a then fervently socialist All Souls historian. Handsome, easily embarrassed, especially by women, uneasily in a middle territory, he played a kind of left hand, right hand game; years afterwards he once quoted to me Auden's early poem of the Thirties:

> I have a handsome profile
> I have been to a great public school
> I've a little money invested
> Then why do I feel such a fool
> As if I owned a world that has had its day?

I'll get a job in the factory/I'll live with factory boys? Well, I will put them on the air. *I'll go out poaching on my own estate?* I will. And of the several kinds of unpeaceful ambivalence in which he lived, one was exemplified in the cult of the poems, half parody, half fear, a quarter rejection, three-quarters regret or nostalgia, of John Betjeman. (More than anyone except Betjeman himself Jim Hughes was responsible for establishing the cult of Betjemania in broadcasting.) For total release he was too caught; for total acceptance, too good, too intelligent, with too sharp a realization of the ridiculous. He inclined Audenwards, but he was to be found searching out F. W. Harvey *(From the troubles of the world/I turn to ducks)* deep in his untidy lawyer's office in the Forest of Dean, and observing on his speaker's card that his scripts were likely to be covered in marmalade.

He tried several ways out of a cocoon woven tightly around himself — at any rate after the death of his widowed mother in 1950. He left his West of England (from which the Broadcasting House at the top of his pseudo-ancestor's Regent

8

Street had so far been unable to drag him) to serve the B.B.C. in Egypt, in India. My God, the poverty, the misery. My God, the English, the chota-peg drinkers. He tried marriage, he tried drink. No good. He was one of those for whom there is no peace, no solution, no absolution; out of which life he wrote (and it seems to me, as I read them, a miracle that my old friend ever came so far into the openness of words) the most honest of his poems, the best things by far that he ever wrote, *Soliloquy at a Masked Ball, The Lone Wolf's Comforter, Epitaph on a Worthless Debauchee, Sentimental Poet, Grazing Rights, I who am not Forgetful, In Time of Disaster* – none of them poems (I think) that he had the nerve to try and publish, all of them personal and painful (though the pain had still to become acute in *Grazing Rights*), yet distanced – himself the actor who remained 'in disciplined burlesque upon the stage', himself Narcissus, in disaster,

> Regretting all of this absurd mistake
> Narcissus peers into the crimson lake,

himself the blind rook:

> The rain beats in the wood; in whipt tree tops
> the nests swim black against the horde of skies.
> From branch to branch the shabby emblem drops.
> The sun comes breaking through. The blind rook dies.

But I think he is bleak, not self-pitiful, in these poems, in the extreme loneliness of his both comfortable and most irksome, most strangling, most uncomfortable cocoon. He was lovable (though if he wanted affection, it could also irritate him); and I thought him less uneasy in his retirement at Keevil, where he no longer had such need at last to project himself in bleak poems; which speak, all the same, for more than himself.

GEOFFREY GRIGSON

RECOLLECTIONS OF PENNETHORNE HUGHES I.

Charles James Pennethorne Hughes was born at Thirlmere, Daniel Street, Ryde, Isle of Wight, on October 29th, 1907. His father was the Reverend Charles Ernest Hughes, M.A. of Keble College, Oxford, who for most of his life was a country vicar, in Yorkshire and finally in Wiltshire. His mother was a Miss Pennethorne, a descendant of Sir James Pennethorne, 1801 to 1871, the architect who completed Carlton House Terrace for John Nash, and laid out New Oxford Street and Endell Street in London, and built the highly successful west wing to Somerset House. Sir James' brother, John Pennethorne, the mathematician and architect, is said first to have discovered the entasis in the Greek column. The Pennethornes were the children of George IV by Mrs John Nash.

C. J. Pennethorne Hughes was generally known as Jim and as 'Pennethorne' by the more pedantic of us, who liked to think of his Royal ancestry. He was at school at Oundle and Captain of Hockey and Boxing, and in 1926 won a History Exhibition to Hertford College, Oxford. Throughout his life he was elegant, slim and unruffled. At Oxford he was a member of a Literary Society called the Mermaid, which brought him into touch with C. S. Lewis and the more serious literary people of his day, such as Geoffrey Grigson and Wystan Auden and Stephen Spender. After obtaining his degree he entered the Great Western Railway as a traffic apprentice and then became a master at Oundle. Here he was a close friend of Arthur Marshall, who was also on the staff there, and had been at school with him, who writes:

'He is happily remembered for his good manners, his wit and his elegance (he was said to possess a dozen smart suits — an unscholastic wardrobe indeed). He had an affectionate if irreverent feeling for his old school and, unlike several of his kind and generation, did not grieve about not having been at Eton. It was always clear that he would not long remain a schoolmaster and was merely looking in on his way to somewhere else. Nevertheless, he was a conscientious and supremely unstuffy teacher and bad temper and unkindness were both quite foreign to his nature.'

In 1935 Pennethorne became a Talks Producer in the liveliest part of the B.B.C., which was and probably still is, the Bristol region. It was the region from which such remarkable producers emerged as Francis Worsley, the inventor of ITMA, and Pennethorne himself, and of course Geoffrey Grigson. His heart was in the West Country, and he liked anything that was local and regional.

As a producer he could put shy people at their ease, deflate the over-confident, kindly and competently, and encourage writers and artists to be enthusiastic about their subjects on the wireless. When war broke out and the Western Region became the headquarters of both religion and variety, Pennethorne much enjoyed their juxtaposition. He was sent as Director of Broadcasting in Cairo, which produced some of his bitterest poems and his most amusing. In 1947 he returned to the London B.B.C. as Director of the Eastern Service.

In about 1950 he was made 'headmaster' as he liked to call himself — for a lot of his analogies came from school — of the Staff Training Department. In this capacity he used to say to trainees, as he handed them the various technical manuals they had to master, 'at this school we give the prizes at the beginning of term instead of at the end'.

From Oxford onwards Pennethorne hid his inner feelings under a mask of wit and satire. The more deeply he felt about something the more he liked to disguise his feelings with humour. Yet he was never jocose.

11

He knew much about witchcraft, ethnology, place names, surnames and English topography. He married in 1948 a Belgian lady whom he had met in Cairo. There were no children and she died in 1961. He was much loved by an intimate few, and much liked by very many. He seemed lonely.

JOHN BETJEMAN

2.

The poet of this book wrote and published under the names of Pennethorne Hughes, C. J. Pennethorne Hughes, James Pennethorne Hughes and Charles Hughes. His consciousness of names was reflected, too, in researches and writing on the subjects of surnames and Christian names. All names, especially his own, were important to him. His mother, the person who made the deepest impression on his life and emotions, always thought, wrote and spoke of him as 'Jim'; at school he was 'Charles,' and he enjoyed being called 'Pennethorne' by his Oxford contemporaries. To him, however, these were not simply period changes; he continued to employ them as plumbing marks between his various activities and depths of involvement.

Like most people, he was composed of several different characters: he was more clearly conscious of the fact than some and, on superficial levels at least, he sometimes was at pains to live out the conflicting personalities separately. This was most apparent in his broadcasting, which he did at his most ambitious standard as Pennethorne Hughes but, in the fields of names, folk lore and language, as Charles Hughes. Sometimes, however, the distinction extended further and deeper: his relationship with a particular person might be deduced by the name with which he signed a letter.

One side of Jim Pennethorne Hughes was almost a caricature of the product of the English public school of the early inter-war period, and the professional middle class; the other was the man of modesty, sharp thought, taste and doubt. He was a good-looking schoolboy, popular, amiable, amusing, successful at games, academically capable enough to win a history exhibition to Hertford College, sufficiently creative to be printed in *Oxford Poetry,* and as steady as required to take a good degree.

He remained personable, tall, strongly built, with a good carriage, clear-lined, patrician features and a fresh complexion. He was an amusing talker, at pains not to overbear or bore; where another person might say 'er' or 'um', he made a joke or an allusion. He observed the code of behaviour of a twentieth century public schoolboy — even while he joked about it — because he saw no alternative which would not offend his taste.

His *1815–1918: The Nineteenth Century and the World War — an Outline of European History,* published in 1935, became a standard school text book; but, surprisingly, he could not be persuaded to revise it after 1945. *While Shepheard's Watched,* an astute and biting study of Egypt, and *Witchcraft,* in which he handled important and faithfully collected material with adroit lightness, and *The Shell Guide to The Isle of Wight* and to *Kent* were those of his books that pleased him most. He mistrusted signs or assumptions of success and needed the constant reassurance of being published by a fresh editor or publisher, or recognised by a new critic, to sustain belief in himself.

His broadcasting was sensitive and skilful: he understood the craft deeply and expertly, and respected it too much to write less than an accomplished script, or on a subject for which he did not feel enthusiasm; his delivery was well inflected; he was a professional broadcaster who never lost his belief in the profession.

Jim Hughes was the best kind of reader, catholic but critical, sensitive, retentive; and he kept every adult book he ever possessed, back to dog-eared copies of the 'Everyman's Library' and Bohn's Classical Library. He collected haphazardly objects that pleased him — chairs, clocks, pottery, prints: he was a pipe-smoker who could not bring himself to throw away a pipe when it became unusable. When his mother died, she still possessed every letter her only son had ever

14

sent her — sometimes two or three a week, from his preparatory school days until her death in the 1950s — and he, for his part, took them and put them with all the letters she had ever sent him.

He could be urbane; for years he was hardly ever seen in London except in the 'uniform' of bowler hat and well-cut, dark overcoat; he always said that he retained his membership of the Bath Club because they cashed his cheques when his bank would not. Given choice, however, he preferred to live in the country, especially Wiltshire, where he spent the vacations of his late teens and early twenties. Those probably were his most impressionable years; he was not only faithful to the setting of them but he remained so to the literary influences of the same time. The authors most completely represented among his books were Wystan Auden, Aldous Huxley, Stephen Spender, John Betjeman and Geoffrey Grigson.

He did not simply camp in a village, he lived in it; he liked village people and talked with them easily. One Whitsun at Keevil he surprised and delighted everyone by turning out for the village cricket team and scoring eighty or so runs in spectacular fashion. He enjoyed the timing of village life: he always became tired early in the evenings, but liked rising early. Most of his writing was done before breakfast and he enjoyed the combination of this habit and his rather ruddy complexion in 'The roseate Hughes of early dawn'. In politics he was a liberal, at a pinch an immovable, though polite, one; in religion he attended the Church of England because it was part of the village, part of the establishment, and because his father was Vicar of Maltby.

By conforming, and through his ability to think and reply quickly and lightly, he contrived in general to avoid committing himself deeply. Yet he was, I imagine, a good school-

15

master, certainly a good head of department, especially of training, because he studied the people under him carefully and sympathetically and worked with genuine goodwill in their interests. Only their gratitude was likely to embarrass him.

He was not reticent with his mother: with anyone else he had to make an effort, usually, one sensed, premeditated, to uncover his feelings. The two decisions which most affected his emotional life were made for non-emotional reasons and he regretted both of them for the rest of his days.

Jim Hughes was gay and erudite; kind, but unwavering in matters concerning his ideals; satirical but understanding; shy and bright; punctilious but questioning; superficially content, yet questing. He cared deeply for traditions, the traditions of people, places, houses: he had a hunger for continuity: he needed more than most the security of marriage and children.

He taught me more than all my schoolmasters; he was kind, convivial and, at times of crisis, clear minded and helpful. There were certain tasks he wished me to discharge after he died; they were small return for all his goodness; they have been done; but I could wish they had been more demanding.

JOHN ARLOTT

THIRTY EIGHT POEMS

by

PENNETHORNE HUGHES

NO SOUL TO SAVE

Shabby coats and licences,
Shall I go by bus or train
or take the car and will it rain?
Tension falters by degrees,
    incentive bogged: no soul to save.

No, listen. Some indifferent tomb
will warehouse my material things.
My bones shall founder with a king's
or ashes dust a throning-room,
    ambition greeted in the grave.

Poor ambition to consort
with such museum recompense.
Stick flags above the known pretence,
the present front: sail into port
    a pilot not a galley-slave.

SOLILOQUY AT A MASKED BALL

(reflectively)   To accept love must be the sin against the Holy Ghost.
Or is the latest balcony the one that bruises most?
Only please leave me: I am not very well
(though not alas with hemlock).
                 Please die, little Nell.
                 Some bird will tell,
(faster)   Leaving thousands to their tears: a *Daily Sketch* deceas
And me to fires eternally, and for the moment, peace.

THE LONE WOLF'S COMFORTER

The Lone Wolf's comforter pants on alone,
baying the moon he can no longer see.
As death winds in the gusts across the sky,
and down there in the valley,
                                        carelessly,
the lone wolves hasten happy to the pack
and raven hungry round the almanack.

High on the hill, blind and without surprise,
the lone wolf's comforter, with bloodshot eyes
coughs half a yelp, shudders his pelt and dies,

and moonbeams thread his sheepshorn memories.

EPITAPH ON A WORTHLESS DEBAUCHEE

He died. The world had cast him off
with a slim shudder of deserved disgust.
He died, regretting only those few years when lust
was wasted as he worshipped sentiment.
He cursed the hours he lingeringly had spent
in doing what seems wise to you and me.
He died: most execrated by the just,
Loved, with a passion very white and high, by three.

SENTIMENTAL POET

Taunted by sparrows, outcast of his tribe,
tattered by beaks, jostled and scarified,
hearing the branches violin a gibe,
a blind rook seeks a harbour or a bride.

Hating the sparrows, hated in his turn,
his bride no mate, with caws about his ears
sightless he wheels away from eyes that burn,
not being too proud but being too old for tears.

The rain beats in the wood; in whipt tree tops
the nests swim black against the horde of skies.
From branch to branch the shabby emblem drops.
The sun comes breaking through. The blind rook dies.

CALL TO PRAYER

God is a scientist, God an engineer,
Trade Unionist, leader with a cheer.
God is a general, God is a god
With beard like Jehovah, sainted and odd
Sitting in stained-glass Valhalla.

God is a trumpet noise, a band
Crooner and college giver of the by by hand,
God is a worker of iron fist,
A bourgeois, a shiny capitalist
Sitting in a giant motor car.

God has many factories and a stadium.
God made love nests, Art, and radium.
His eye, his hem, his shield is wide,
From him no cog can ever hide
In all Relativia.

God is vitality, punch and pep:
God is human ideology in step,
God is the sacred universal head.
Or God is a smell, long dead.

I WHO AM NOT FORGETFUL

I, who am not forgetful, never remember you,
You, who were always within my horizon,
Like some well-known tree, some Georgic, limited view,
Known and absorbed, but not pondered or dwelt on.
But sometimes, when I seem to see your hands
Making little movements over the tired, worn skirt,
Then, for half a moment, the people, the storm sands
Recede, and I feel hurt.
And I half remember, and look in your eyes,
Until some voice forbids: forbidden
By tongues, I let my words stay unsaid, hidden.
But understand; and do not lonely bear
A numbness, that I do not care.
I care, though I do not remember you.

IN TIME OF DISASTER

The actor shows great courage to remain
in disciplined burlesque upon the stage,
when at the FIRE! the audience have all fled.
Some cunning ones to smash a window pane,
not stifle where the panic mothers rage,
and scarleted commissionaires lie dead.

Regretting all of this absurd mistake
Narcissus peers into the crimson lake.

SEPTEMBER 1941

These are the last days, the first days: yet the bees
submerge the throbbing engines: bunching trees
in dark perspective on the Mendip slopes
absorb the senses. There comes a fingering breeze.
These are the last days, the last hopes.

Death breaks in the Dnieper valley. Men die in the air, at sea.
Here we are set among their dreams: note how delightfully
the red-roof coven of the village lies
haze-hung between the valley's green, as we
half hear the hum of heartbreak in the skies.

The earth smells up towards September. Birth
lies in the ground and stirs beneath the green.
These are the first days of the earth,
we are the blood that lies between
the first days and the last. When we have been,
its richness still will supersede the dearth,
watch death revolve, but harvests intervene.

PROVINCIAL

He smudged the roofs with sentimental rose,
saw painted smoke across a fading sky;
an abbey and a paragon he chose,
a train with pennoned puffs went by.

The Crimson Talons of her hand
were well perceived by that obscure young man
who monotoned some too-indulgent wand
to make her his and metropolitan.

They pricked the dusk with rather amber lights,
the hush and history breathed towards the stars.
He donned his Hamlet-haunted tights
and sought for metaphysics in the bars.

An old dervish, the ghaffir of Gizeh,
not so much whirling as turning and turning in measures,
one arm receiving, the other submissive,
there in the incense
whilst the drums beat.

And the drums beat in successive repetitive
bloodrhythm as the heads nod:
the swaying sheikh with the censer
breathed on the coals, and the incense
clouded the khaki American visitors

and the phoney was the phoney
and the dervishes thrumbed
and the ghaffir of Gizeh was twirling twirling
round in a measure of measureless memory
there in the pillars, the lights and the music,
the Americans, history, the Prophet and Paradise.

And the music stopped
and the ghaffir went back to his place

and we prayed.

Ghaffir: village watchman

LAST LINES

by a little English girl, lately half converted by her nanna to
the faith of Islam, dying of hookworm in the Victoria
Hospital, Cairo.

Give my sandshoes to the boab,
Rubber-ribbed and leather-laced,
For I meet a greater Boab
Who has keys about his waist.

See that Yimkin gets his walkies,
Bread-and-milk upon the floor.
Say the little Sitt is resting
Not that she has Gone Before.

No more I shall see the khamsin;
Hear the cries of Ramadan;
Hear the happy altercation
With the Friday laundry-man;

See Gezira in the floodlight,
Hear my pappa in the bar;
Galabiehs in the gloaming:
Bab-el-Louk by trolley-car.

For the last time, dear Suffragi,
Draw the white mosquito net,
As the Nile, its bale bilharzia,
Oceanwards beats violet.

Only tell them I am sleeping
(Light, please, I can hardly see.
Little Abdul, cease your weeping.)
Wog of Wogs, I come to Thee.

Boab: door-keeper. Sitt: mistress of the house. Khamsin: strong dust-bearing wind from the desert. Galabieh: the long typical Egyptian dress, like a nightshirt. Bilharzia: the hookworm disease affecting some 90 per cent of the fellaheen.

FELLOW GUEST

Chickens in Cairo sometimes are plucked alive
To catch the market in the big hotels.
It helps to keep them, and by showing drive
The farmer thus his few piastres swells.
Some brief repugnance is however found
In guests by whom this painful thing is seen
Which to their kindness greatly does redound.

Come, Pasha, let's go pluck some fellaheen.

POPULATION PROBLEM

Ill fares the land, each smart inverter says,
Where men accumulate and wealth decays.

Poor Egypt, where they both accumulate,
The poor grow poorer, whilst the rich inflate!
Both millionaires and births grow yearly more,
The Nileside flats build on another floor
And prayers alone sustain the sweltering poor.

No village is deserted, all expand
With flyblown children and the windblown sand,
As towns throw out new suburbs to contain
The beys who batten on the cheaply slain.

THE PASHA ANSWERS

I am a pasha: Allah likes a winner.
I also help the poor.
              Pray come to dinner.
My wife is still away: she is in Paris.
There's compensation, though, for one who marries,
And we will find some girls and some champagne
And turn the Nile into the shining Seine.
Be sure you'll come? You will? That is a date.

On Tuesday we will visit my estate.

DEDICATION CEREMONY

For forty-three years he played with a straight bat,
he taught *Punch* to eleven generations.
With wheezy emphasis explaining that
England was the best and greatest of the nations.

For forty-three years he taught about God,
Reporting the Bearded One with cricket stories,
With kindly chuckle and with kindly prod
And sex-advice. O deary, O tempores.

He died, and then a rather ugly font
Was dedicated to him, quite sincerely
By all the followers of *Punch*. They don't
Remember him. He was a nice man, really.

IN NO DISRESPECT OF DOCTOR ARNOLD

My good name holds: I play the rules,
my talk is like a sewer.
I represent the Public Schools
because my heart is pure.
Because my heart is pure, brave boys,
because my heart is pure,
I know that clever men are fools
because my heart is pure.

But what became of it at last?
quoth Little Peterkin.
But Pan was dead, and gods were past,
the shades of blight were falling fast,
men had the Will to Win.
Because your hearts are pure, brave boys,
you have the will to win, brave boys,
so duck that dirty Peterkin,
because your tarts are pure.

RETIREMENT

The parakeets obey the sun,
The ants obey the sand,
The timeless minutes silken run
Toward the hour hand.
The figures silent hover by,
Obedient to the word.
The sky scorching panoply.
No single bird.

No movement in the static sheer
Of Bikaneer.

Can I forget, who here am set
In tepid-tempered Junes,
The memory of tiger nights,
And golden afternoons?

THE RAJ

The Taj stands firm,
The Raj does not,
It's dismal, dank, Hindu and hot.
While chotah-pegs
Go to the legs
Of Lancers without lances,
A famine pall
Occludes Bengal;
And Congress never dances.

RING OUT, DEAR BELLS

The old believe, the old can still remain.
The young don't mind: it keeps the old in peace.
We only look for what we cannot find,
and, finding not, accept our just release.

But do not fear that standards stay the same:
renounce all progress talk, grudge cheaply change.

The mote within another eye is gone,
but so's the moated grange.

Ring out, dear bells, until the bell-rope rots.

THE URANIUM AGE

The Golden Age, the Golden Age!
Which was, and is to come . . . .
The pinchbeck Present shudders
At prospect of uranium.

The rest is silence.

JEW SÜSS (a synopsis)

In periwig and patch
A mottled crew,
Slow drip the kings and queens and knaves. We watch
That odd ragout.
The puppets puff and clasp their hands
And toss great heads in long to-do.

Apart, stands one who understands,
And, understanding, waits:
                              the Jew.

SAND CASTLE

In the great house the old man still lived on,
coughing amongst the glass-house passages,
whilst house-trained villagers in uniforms
dumb-footed followed his insistent bells.
The kitchen supped to magic saxophones
with muffled microphone behind baize doors:
the upper picture-frames lipped dust.
The peaches grew the loveliest tissue gowns,
the frailest frocks for the head-gardener's Rose.

Out in the park the froglike little girls
rose on the lower branches of the trees
and once a year the pink hunt roaring came
and shouted at the wispy man
propped safe and ulstered on the straddling steps.

Saxophones off, the house creaked death
and some discomfort through the night
and once a month the rector came to tea.

LULLABY

Beyond the elms are even colder stars
of an untalking grim frigidity,
who eye with weary stare the falcate moon
and do not heed stale Mars' celestial wars.
They burn in hard undim rigidity;
and peacefully.
    This pocket of the earth
seems older, colder, clearer than those stars,
as you are nearer, dearer, than the moon.
Tremble then, idolist, tremble then happily.

LINES TO J.B.

On First Looking into 'New Lights for Old Chancels'

Miss B. 'I'm sure that it's a Betjeman!
    See how he does the hair.
Besides, the tenderness he has
    In that plantation there!'

Mrs R. 'No.*That* is not a Betjeman,
    The whole idea is dirty.
I'd say it was a Pennethorne
(The man who wrote *No Bishop's Pawn*)
    And not the bearded Betjeman —'
(together)   'The son of elder Betjeman—'
Mrs R.   '. . . touched up in nineteen thirty.'

Mr R. 'As Dr Grigson indicates
    in that expensive book,
The last thing you must look for
    is the kind of way things look.
All these fellows have a sort
    of — well, of lack of grit.
But Betjeman's the worst because
    of course he started it.

They're all the same, and what is more
    it's damned unhealthy, I
Confess that I'm a modern
    and I like to laugh, or cry.'*

Miss B.   'But if it *is* a Betjeman,
      Which I don't think, don't you?
It must be most *expensive* . . . '

Mr & Mrs R.   'Ah, that's true.'

Spirit of
Pity   So found no school, Remote, remain
A transfer on a hidden window-pane,
That none can find who fail with crumpled dress
To storm the flower-house through the Wilderness
Nor hear Nostalgia creak across the strand,
The trams and teas of vanished Metroland.
          (fade up Vespers)

He means that he belonged to the New Heart movement of the early nineteen-sixties, already of course superseded by the Bexhill school.

HEDGES

By the mercy of God and thick hedges
Hidden from remoter spots
(In one of which I lie, tossing
An acorn cup) fly hideous obscene
Motors, hooting
A path to London, where they may
Once more forget
They are in England,
And can read the *Daily Mail* and the poems of Osbert Sitwell, and
                    see some shows and see one another
And then
    go for a real rest
To Brighton or to
Cannes.

Thank God for thick
Hedges.

CLERGY PENSION LIST
or A Long Trip To The Seaside

King's School, Keble, Cuddesdon,
Laburnums by the lock,
With ivy by the summer-house
And holy hollyhock

Hot fêtes upon the patient lawn,
With bowling for the pig:
The Easter congregation small
Although the takings big.

The early work in Maida Vale,
The curacy at Ryde,
Then Surrey (smart) and Hallam (not)
And rectories beside:

Hymns and bells and Sunday School
And visiting the sick,
With people's wardens who would think
My deafness was a trick.

King's School, Keble, Cuddesdon,
Hymns and bells and tea,
And money troubles and at last
Saint Leonards, by the sea.

THE BODY'S BOOK

The mysteries grow in the soul,
The body's book finds ready sale,
The publishers take happy toll,
The sheets unfold their scrabbled tale:
Between the bawds the issues pale.

Editions hot from every press,
The pop-eyed readers' ready laugh,
With stable-mannered maladdress
Each sporty little centre-half
Explores again the fatted calf.

The mysteries grow in the soul
But yet the body is his book,
And tears extend from pole to pole,
From Ivy Dene to Nonie's Nook,
At liberties the author took.

HARVEST FESTIVAL

Seasonally they lay beetroot on the head
Of the recumbent abbot's majesty,
While harvest after harvest loaves of bread
Are hallowed by his grim vicinity.
The new, fat, plum-faced vicar comes,
And his infuriating wife.
He twirls ingratiating thumbs;
His furthest terror is parochial strife.
His wife has little angry eyes,
And mutters at good, friendly Mrs Rands.
She needs less tea and much more exercise,
Having bunched clothes, and silly, busy hands.
      The vicar, coming, lays with clammy palm
A clean potato on the abbot's breast.
His wife with a tomato spoils the calm
And wrecks the joy of the abbatial rest.

      Where the bells sound clear on misty eves,
Thorold of Feschamp sleeps unstirred.
With banks of reminiscent leaves
Lanes are still leafy where he spurred.

      Thorold lies lost in the embracing ground,
The abbot lies insulted in the nave.
He feels parochial fingers fidget round.

      Why is it Earnest People can't behave?

REVIVAL

(dim) The leaves are Mariana in the spring,
       among the elms the church is grey.
       Victorian crows are on the lazy wing,
(pp) yellow the hay.

(cr) Pre-Raphaelite are certain plants,
       distinct each fact but blurred the whole.
       The choir ignores the newer chants,
       eyes faithful on the aureole.

                  (Break step over the bridge, then)

(ff) Happy days are here again,
              upholstery in green:
(p) with solemn and not sickly pain.
              (ff) God save the Queen!

ON BATHING WITH DULCIE

Aphrodite of the South Coast,
Helen of the shops and strands,
old the charms your lips and mouth boast,
Timeless your pale present hands.
Immemorial your tresses,
and your trite inviting eyes,
known the kisses sun impresses,
when you bathe in Paradise.
When you bathe, like any typist,
when you giggle by the groyne
Pan recalls where lips were ripest,
Satyrs glimpse a Grecian loin.
Timeless woman, Aphrodite,
Helen, Helen in the main.

Come and have a dive with Dulcie.
Golly, she's a spanking jane!

Relativity, and History. Don't we, don't we make a fuss!
What a lot of fun the gods had. What a lot of fun for us!
(Sang the sea-soaked poetaster, bathing with his stimulus.)

GRAZING RIGHTS

'Herrick's Lalage with cow-like eyes
was sister, sweet, to you,
with orbs so soft in round surprise,
so fatuously blue.
Seductive cow, so innocent
of sophistry: dear meat,
may I not share your fair content,
your lushy meadowsweet?'

'No: for you have a butcher look
most red and indiscreet.'

LOVE SCENE ON THE PROMENADE

The percept and the concept were walking hand in hand.
I loved them as I saw them, and I told them of my love.
And the concept (she was lovely) drew me nearer, as I'd planned,
and her eyes could understand me, and she loved me for my love.
But the percept (she was lovely) shook her head upon my love.
She flirted. 'Don't be naughty: come and listen to the band.'
— The last walk together, on the promenade, at Hove —
So I buried pretty concept, in the quantities of sand.

TIME STAGGERS ON

Time staggers on, but new communications
Only serve to cater for the recognised sensations,
Everything's a matter of degree,
All ideas have got a pedigree.
Though we're smart, the end's as long in coming,
Progress only seems to mean a different kind of plumbing
Drumming
      out what it's so plain to see:
What man is, man will always be.

The waist line and the nations,
Each may rise and fall,
Gossip snips be written up
By Swift or Donegal,
But underneath the skin the old blood's running after all,
      Though Time may stagger on.

The minuet may vanish
But let us do the Yam,
Horoscopes are all the go
Though Druids were a sham.
Museums had the stage-coach once but now it is the tram,
      So Time may stagger on.

They thought that power politics
      Were really very good
When man had still a hairy tail,
      Was not out of the wood.
         And look where the sub-men have gone!

(They're quite big boys now)
The problem and the passions
On the endless chain,
Fashions boomerang us back,
Here we are again!
They've speeded up the airways, but there's always Charles's Wain,
    Though Time may stagger on.

THERE'S NO FIRST CLASS TO HEAVEN

Have you got your tickets?
Have you got your furs?
Step into the bar and meet the other passengers,
All the folks are cheering on the quay
But the stewards look rather fishy and their manner's rather free,
It doesn't seem at all like pleasure cruising.

You may buy your way to a Tatler success
By the sit of your eyebrows, the cut of your dress,
But you can't grease the slipway to Happiness,
           There's no first class to Heaven.

You may score full marks by your fashion-plate hips,
Dorchester teeth or advertisement lips,
But you can't bribe Charon — he doesn't take tips,
           There's no first class to Heaven.

Goodbye limousine, milk and honeyland,
Soon there'll be an end, silk and moneyland,
Goodbye caviare, cars and Claridges,
Goodbye lovers and goodbye marriages.
        (Marriages are made in Heaven)

Though you follow the fashion from Goodwood to Cannes
In eternal pursuit of the *live*-year plan,
You can't cheat that one-way ferryman,
           There's no first class to Heaven!

Who has seen my valet?
Is my luggage in the hold?
There doesn't seem much service and it's really very cold,
Look at those odd people on the deck,
The captain can't talk English and he will not change my cheque,
Tell me now why did we come along?
Listen what a dreary note that gloomy landing gong!

You may buy your way to a paragraph fame
By your Cartier bills and your grandfather's name,
But you can't buy Peter — he isn't the same,
    There's no first class to Heaven.

You may get front seats for the best of the fun
At polo or Lords or the new Cresta run.
When it comes to the end, though, you've only begun,
    There's no first class to Heaven.

Goodbye manicure, modes and Molyneux's,
Soon you'll have to pay all your folly dues,
Goodbye kisses in quiet localities
Where no chaperone, maid, or valet is.
    (You gotta behave in Heaven)

All those Embassy girls of notorious charm
Will still get their dancing: no need for alarm,
But it's hard to fox-trot to a harp and a psalm,
    There's no first class to Heaven!

SIDEWALK SILHOUETTE

Folded in an ermine, sweet
passion flower of Jermyn Street,
I can see you scarlet toed,
fragile line of Freud and Spode,
infinitely undistressed
by homilies of what is Best,
infinitely undismayed
by accident of life, afraid
only of an errant gust
unsettling the golden dust
that makes your corrugated head,
moulded soft and filleted,
fluted trim and mounted brave,
shimmer like a cornfield wave.
I can see those baby eyes
insolent in their surprise,
windows through which light is shed
to that darling vacant head.
Aphrodite from the sea.
What a change from Bermondsey!
How wise to make your bed another's,
not share it with two younger brothers,
scrub the floors and clean the sink,
watching father in his drink,
watching mother cough and die,
and that bloody baby cry.

Or, as you sip the cigarettes,
do you sometimes have regrets,
and as you idly sup and sip,
creamy throated, think a bit?

Ask for bread, men give you stones,
diamonds and overtones.

SONG WITH A MORAL

By the Horrid Stranger

Wine maketh old wives wenches,
  Wine washeth off the daub,
Fills hearts and empties benches.
  Drink all ye can absorb,
    brave boys,
  Drink all ye can absorb.

Wine warms ye in the morning,
  Is kind to ye at night.
But heed my solemn warning:
  Be sure ye cork it tight,
    brave boys,
  Be *sure* ye cork it tight.

I knew a man loved wine, once,
  More than a fish loves sea.
For the sake of old lang syne, once,
  He drank a glass with me,
    brave boys,
  A glass (or two) with me.

CLOWN'S SONG

I am a scullion Mercury
    unlimbered by the gods.
The peas run over my hands, and leave
    me staring at the pods.
The Heavens' drunken messenger,
    I titter at the sea
which rolls unspent; but shingle beds
    scream laughter back at me.
Around my head, in gay cascades
    the centuries are furled,
but I remain, with careless hair
Diana's laughing solitaire,
the playboy of the silver stair,
    the mopsy of the world.